Cornerstones of Freedom

Medicine in the American West

LUCILE DAVIS

CHILDREN'S PRESS®
A Division of Scholastic Inc.
New York • Toronto • London • Auckland • Sydney
Mexico City • New Delhi • Hong Kong
Danbury, Connecticut

Reading Consultant: **Linda Cornwell, Coordinator of School Quality and
Professional Improvement, Indiana State Teachers Association**

Library of Congress Cataloging-in-Publication Data

Davis, Lucile.
   Medicine in the American West / Lucile Davis.
      p. cm.—(Cornerstones of freedom)
   Includes index.
   ISBN 0-516-22004-7 (lib. bdg.)   0-516-25958-X (pbk.)
1. Medicine—West (U.S.)—History—19th century—Juvenile literature.
[1. Medicine—West (U.S.)—History—19th century.] I. Title. II. Series.

R154.5.W47 D38 2001
610'.978'09034—dc21
                         00-031608

GROLIER
PUBLISHING

In 1803, the United States bought a large piece of land from France that lay west of the Mississippi River. The territory was about 800,000 square miles (2,100,000 square kilometers). This land deal was known as the Louisiana Purchase.

President Thomas Jefferson supported Americans moving into the land west of the Mississippi—the American West. A study of population growth in the United States stated the number of people in the new nation would double every twenty-three years. The president knew the United States could support a larger population if there were enough farmers and farmland. The Louisiana Purchase provided the land, but few Americans would survive there without better medical practices.

The Louisiana Purchase gave American pioneers the opportunity to move west of the Mississippi River.

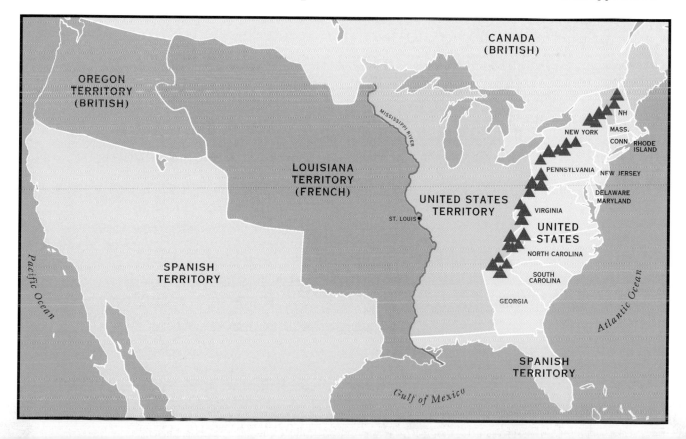

William Clark

Meriwether Lewis

President Jefferson knew medical practices in the United States needed improvement. He appointed Captains Meriwether Lewis and William Clark to explore the American West and find a waterway to the Pacific Ocean. He wanted the Lewis and Clark Expedition to have the best medical knowledge and equipment available. The explorers were given a large medicine chest containing the best medical tools and medicines available. Captain Lewis went to Philadelphia. He learned first aid and received advice from Dr. Benjamin Rush, the leading doctor in the United States at that time. But medical practices in the United State were not very effective and often deadly.

Doctors in the United States practiced medicine in the same way doctors in Europe had for centuries. They treated people based on the theory of the four humors, or liquid elements of the body. These elements were blood, phlegm (thick matter coughed up during a cold), yellow bile, and black bile. Doctors thought people became ill when their elements were out of balance.

To cure a patient's illness, a doctor tried to balance the person's elements. Depending on the patient's symptoms, the doctor usually ordered one or more treatments—bleeding, blistering, purging (cleaning out the intestines), vomiting, and sweating. Doctors believed bleeding relieved a fever because this treatment eased the pressure on the veins of the body. They applied hot plasters to cause skin blisters that would supposedly rid the body of unclean elements. Purging and vomiting were the treatments doctors recommended when they thought patients had too much yellow and black bile. Sweating, it was believed, cleared the body of any other unclean elements.

This 1804 cartoon shows a doctor bleeding a patient.

The medical theory of the four humors was wrong. The treatments for balancing the humors did not cure illnesses and often killed the patients. So when Lewis and Clark headed west, their medical knowledge was limited. Like the pioneers who would follow them, the captains and their company would discover new medical treatments as well as new territory.

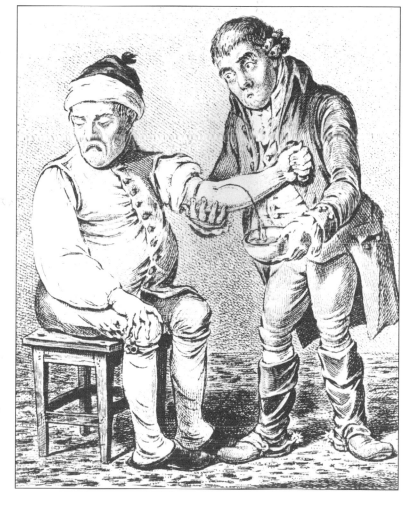

On May 14, 1804, the Lewis and Clark Expedition left St. Louis, Missouri, and traveled northwest. Lewis kept a journal of the new plants and animals he saw along the way. He also gained information about the healing qualities of some of these plants.

In this journal entry, Lewis describes a plant.

This information came from some of the American Indians he met.

One winter, Lewis and Clark camped among the Mandan Indians. They met a fifteen-year-old Shoshone woman named Sacagawea. When the expedition left the Mandan camp, Sacagawea went with them. She helped them obtain supplies, lodging, and medical assistance from her people and the Nez Perce Indians.

The discovery of American Indian medical practices and medicinal plants, the well-equipped medicine chest, and Captain Lewis's training helped the explorers survive the journey. Although no doctor went along, only one person on the expedition died. They returned to St. Louis on September 23, 1806.

Sacagawea was one of the Lewis and Clark Expedition's guides, and she translated their requests for assistance to the Shoshone and Nez Perce Indians.

Even before Lewis and Clark returned, pioneers were rolling past St. Louis into the American West. The people heading west were not as well equipped as the Lewis and Clark Expedition. But like the explorers, the pioneers took what medical knowledge and medicine they had available and learned to make do along the way. Some doctors moved to the American West, but most wagon trains did not have a doctor traveling with them. With so few people in such a huge territory, pioneers needed to be able to do a number of jobs well. Although trained doctors were scarce, people shared their medical experiences with one another.

This late 1800s photograph shows Catherine Skinner, a midwife from central Colorado.

Elizabeth Perry was such a person. She was a bride traveling with her husband to the Oregon territory. She was only seventeen, but she studied medicinal herbs and had a gift for healing. She tended the sick and delivered babies. When she reached what is now Oregon, she raised a family and practiced medicine.

Most pioneer women took recipe books to the American West. These books contained recipes for cooking and herbal remedies for pain, fever, and other illnesses. Some women, like Elizabeth Perry, became experienced in delivering babies. Known as midwives, these

An advertisement for Ayer's Cherry Pectoral, one of many medicines that were supposed to cure coughs

women also had some knowledge of women's diseases and how to treat them.

Some wagon masters had medical experience as well as knowledge of western trails. Sol Tetherow was a wagon master on the Oregon Trail who had a collection of medical recipes for treating wounds and soothing fevers. His most requested recipe was for a cough syrup made from licorice root and a herb known as balm of Gilead. A child with a cough could keep the entire wagon train up at night. The syrup stopped the cough and helped everyone get a good night's sleep.

Life on a wagon train was dangerous. Wild animals, disease-carrying insects, and unknown poisonous plants could kill without warning. Native tribes, angered by the invasion of their land, attacked the wagon trains. However, accidents were the leading cause of death for people heading west. Many people drowned or died from accidental gunshot wounds.

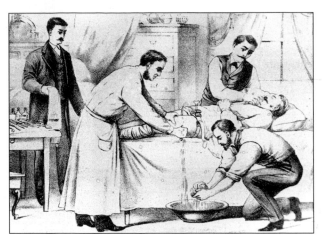

This illustration shows a doctor amputating a man's leg.

Without a doctor or hospital nearby, pioneers had to rely on one another and make do with the talents and tools available. One pioneer's accident illustrates how medicine was practiced in the American West. The pioneer had spotted a wolf trailing the wagon train. The man reached for his rifle, but it was stuck in the back of his wagon. As he pulled the gun out, muzzle first, the trigger caught. The gun fired, shattering the man's upper arm. The wagon master said the arm could not be saved. It would have to be amputated, or cut off.

The man stretched out on the prairie grass as some people from the wagon train prepared to operate. A hunter brought out his skinning knife. A teamster, a person who drove one of the wagons, sharpened the teeth in his saw. Several people removed a large bolt from one of the wagons. Tail-end first, the iron bolt was placed in a roaring fire. The hunter tied a rope tightly around the man's arm to stop the flow of blood.

A dozen people held the injured man down while the hunter did his work. After he amputated the man's arm, the hunter burned the open wound with the hot iron bolt to stop the bleeding. The hunter covered the wound with grease and bandaged it with cloth. The man lived through the operation without benefit of an anesthetic, a gas or liquid drug given to someone before an operation to prevent pain. He eventually recovered.

The man's experience was painful, but he could not have received better treatment from an experienced doctor. Lack of medical education was part of the problem. In the early 1800s, there were no standards for medical training. People who wanted to study medicine became apprentices. An apprentice paid an experienced doctor for the opportunity to clean the doctor's office, mix medicines, and help during surgeries. The apprentice read the doctor's books about medical practices. This training might last from a few months to three years.

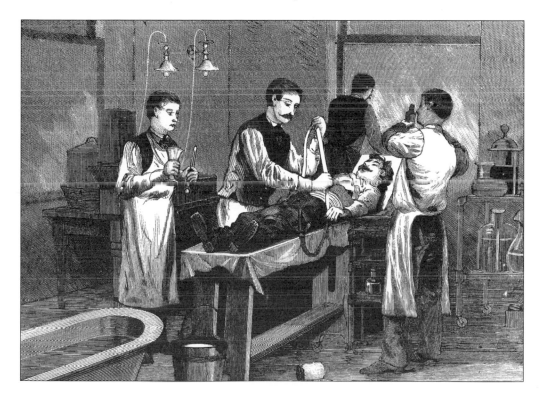

In this drawing, the person on the far left is an apprentice. He is assisting a doctor during surgery.

When their apprenticeship ended, many apprentices went to medical school. During the early 1800s, medical schools did not offer an excellent education. Most schools had classrooms but no laboratories. Few medical schools had libraries, and if they did, there were not many books. The school year for medical students usually lasted only three to four months—from late November to early March. Most medical schools required two years of study, but before 1850, medical students repeated their first-year courses during the second year. Then the students graduated and could practice medicine.

In this 1892 photograph, doctors show medical students, including a few women, how to perform surgery.

Many trained doctors practiced medicine but rarely performed surgery. Few doctors had the education, experience, or skill to operate. Most doctors paid little attention to keeping their surgical instruments free of germs, so cutting into a patient was dirty, dangerous, and deadly. Most patients died within days of an operation due to infections in their surgical wounds.

It was difficult for universities to provide students with surgical training and experience. Universities offered courses in anatomy, the study of the human body. However, most universities could not offer a laboratory course to help students gain experience operating on a human. A laboratory course required a dead body to study, and most communities objected for religious reasons to students cutting on the dead. With little practical experience, even trained doctors had to learn as they practiced medicine. In the American West, learning to make do with the tools available turned into medical discoveries.

A doctor in Oregon discovered cow's milk helped cowboys soothe pains in their stomachs. Another Oregon doctor invented a surgical tool out of a thimble to reduce the pressure on the brain of a boy who had been kicked in the head by a horse. A Texas doctor discovered Plaster of Paris held pieces of broken bone in place while it healed.

Although these discoveries added new treatments and tools to the field of medicine, few doctors wanted to move to the American West. Doctors could not make a living in the sparsely populated area. After the pioneers found a place to live, they spread out over hundreds of miles. Each family staked a claim to a number of acres of land. They worked hard to clear the land, plant crops, or raise cattle. They had little or no money. Doctors in the American West often traded their medical services for a sack of grain or a live chicken.

Few doctors wanted to practice medicine in the American West because it was difficult to make a living in this sparsely populated region.

Because there were so few doctors in the American West, people asked other professionals for medical assistance. Dentists were often called on to treat injuries and illnesses. Pharmacists mixed and sold medicines and operated general stores. When there was no doctor, pharmacists prescribed medicines for injuries and illnesses. Pioneers survived, in part, by having many skills and helping others to learn them.

Even trained doctors found they needed to have many skills to make a living in the American West. One of these doctors was Dr. William Worrall Mayo. Born in England, he began his medical training there before sailing for the United States. In the United States, he became the apprentice of a doctor in New York. In 1854, he earned a medical degree then moved to the Minnesota Territory. Mayo found he did more farming than doctoring. People often called him to treat a cow or a horse rather than a human.

Dr. William Worrall Mayo

Dr. Mayo kept a small office in his home for many years. Some patients came to see him, but most of the time he went to the patients. Many doctors in the American West made house calls because it was difficult for pioneers to leave their farms.

Saddlebags

Mortar and pestle

When doctors traveled, they carried their tools and medicines in saddlebags. These saddlebags were specially made. The bags consisted of two leather pouches connected by a wide leather strap that fit across a saddle. The pouches had pockets for carrying small bottles of medicine. The medicines came in powder, liquid, ointment, and pill form. The bags also held a small metal weighing scale for measuring medicine and a mortar and pestle. The pestle was a small-handled tool with a large round end that ground the medicine. The mortar was a bowl-shaped container that held the mixture.

Very few medicines came ready to use. Doctors bought the medicinal ingredients by the pound and measured out doses using the tip of a knife.

If two or more medicines were needed, they were ground together in the mortar. Then the mixture was rolled into a pill. When doctors ran out of these medicines, they would use cures made from plants. Like Captain Lewis, these doctors kept journals noting the discovery of new plants and their healing qualities.

In addition to holding cures and medicines, the saddlebags held a surgery box. This box contained surgical tools such as a cutting knife, lance, and forceps. A lance was used to open boils. The blade of a lance was longer and thinner than the blade of a cutting knife. Forceps were a scissorslike tool used to grasp and hold objects during surgery.

Other items in these saddlebags included sponges, plasters, a heating iron, and a tourniquet. Doctors used sponges to wash wounds or wipe away blood during an operation. A plaster was a treated cloth placed over a wound. The cloth contained a hard substance such as wax to protect the wound as it healed. The heating iron burned an open wound to stop it from bleeding. Doctors also stopped bleeding with a tourniquet. It was a strong leather strap and wooden rod. The doctor wrapped the strap around an injured arm or leg and tied it in a knot. The wooden rod was inserted in the knot and twisted to keep the strap tight around the arm or leg to cut off the flow of blood.

Although many doctors in the American West carried their office in their saddlebags and had few patients, doctors in California faced the opposite problem. In 1848, the discovery of gold in California sent fortune hunters rushing to the state. By the 1850s, tent cities had sprung up close to the gold mines. Fifteen hundred doctors traded their medical tools for pick-axes and tin pans to search for gold. Some of these doctors discovered they could collect more gold by treating miners' injuries and illnesses. These doctors set up offices in tents.

Injuries from accidents and fights kept mining doctors busy, but the worst medical problem they faced was disease. The dirty, over-crowded mining camps were breeding grounds for disease. People in warmer camps were constantly fighting the fevers brought on by insect bites. For instance, miners bitten by ticks often developed Rocky Mountain spotted fever—known as the black measles. Pneumonia and other respiratory diseases were common medical problems in northern mining camps. In such unhealthy environments, miners easily caught contagious diseases such as measles, mumps, and smallpox. There were no cures for these diseases, but doctors could treat the symptoms and keep patients comfortable until they got better or died.

This illustration shows people panning for gold near tent cities in California during the Gold Rush.

Contagious diseases were also a big problem for military doctors. During the American Civil War (1861–1865), more soldiers died of contagious diseases than from war wounds. Military doctors had few trained people to care for the sick and perform surgeries. Because medical help was in short supply, women were called on to fill the need. Although women were once banned from attending medical school, they began to study medicine. Women trained to become doctors and nurses. Civil War doctors and nurses gained skill as surgeons and learned that cleanliness reduced infections. In 1865, the Civil War ended. Some military doctors and nurses moved to the American West for land and opportunity. They taught others what they had learned about surgeries and diseases.

This 1863 photograph shows a surgical tent at Gettysburg, Pennsylvania, during the Civil War.

When regular doctors or nurses could not provide a cure, some people in the American West turned to irregular doctors. Irregular doctors did not follow the standard medical practices of the day. They used common sense and learned from many different kinds of medical practices. Some irregular doctors prescribed herbal cures. Many people preferred these natural remedies to the harsh bleeding and purging prescribed by regular doctors. Some irregular doctors prescribed hot baths. One doctor in Texas ordered mud baths for his patients.

Anyone in the American West could give medical advice and prescribe medicine because the law did not require training to practice medicine. In Galveston, Texas, one so-called doctor offered only one cure to his patients. It was opium, a powerful but dangerous drug. He gave such a large amount of opium to a cowboy that the young man appeared to die. Friends gave the young man a last shave and haircut and wrapped him for burial. They laid him out in an upstairs room, then they gathered downstairs to comfort each other. Hours later, they heard a hard thump followed by mumbling coming from upstairs. The weak cowboy wobbled down the steps. He pointed to his mouth as if asking for a drink. The room cleared in an instant. The young cowboy had lived through the drug overdose.

This illustration is from a children's book that illustrates the letter Q.

Many people did not live to tell others about bad medical treatments. People who pretended to have medical knowledge or skill were called quacks. Quacks operated throughout the United States. Their main objective was money, not a medical cure. Many quacks traveled with medicine shows and sold patent medicines, remedies that they had obtained the right to make, use, and sell.

A medicine show was a troupe of traveling entertainers. They traveled in large wagons painted bright colors and drawn by horses wearing harnesses decorated with bells and tassels. Medicine shows were more entertainment than medicine. The object was to make money, not to cure illness. One historian writes the medicine shows sold "hope in a bottle."

The lead entertainer in a medicine show was the so-called doctor. These entertainers created imaginative tales about their lives. They told stories of having lived with American Indians and learned their medical secrets. The secret usually came in the form of a bottled tonic, a so-called medicine that was supposed to make people feel stronger or better. During the show,

In this illustration of a medicine show, the person blowing the horn is announcing the arrival of the doctor.

American Indians in colorful costumes danced or performed mysterious rituals. Witnesses told the audience the tonic had cured them. The lead entertainer would then appear and supposedly cure a number of people. The people cured were actors from the traveling troupe pretending to be members of the audience.

After the so-called cures, members of the audience lined up to buy a bottle of the magical tonic for fifty cents or one dollar. These tonics did not really cure people. Tonics were often some combination of mineral oil, alcohol, and a little flavoring. These tonics contained ten to twenty-five percent alcohol. The alcohol kept the patient comfortably drowsy or asleep while nature took its course.

How many bottles of tonic the medicine show sold depended on their lead entertainers. Many of these so-called doctors dressed in wild costumes, and they had methods to attract crowds. One of these entertainers was J.I. Lighthall, better known as the Diamond King. He had many costumes. His most impressive costume was a diamond-covered, ankle-length sealskin coat and a wide-brimmed sealskin hat. To attract an audience, the Diamond King offered to pull teeth for free. As he sold his tonic, he kept the bills but threw the change into the crowd. Another entertainer wore buckskins and had a small, pointed beard and long mustache. This made him look like the famous Colonel Buffalo Bill Cody.

Unlike medicine show entertainers, patent medicine salespeople did not travel with a group. They traveled alone or with one assistant. These salespeople traveled in small wagons and sold medicines. Patent medicines came in several forms—pills, ointments, and elixirs. The colorful labels on the medicine bottles listed the diseases the pill, ointment, or elixir cured. What the labels did not describe was how to use the medicine. The patent medicine salespeople would tell of miracle cures brought about by the medicines they sold. If asked, the salespeople gave advice on when and how to take the medicine. People died waiting for the miracle cure.

This 1840 drawing shows a patent medicine salesperson selling his medicine.

Dr. Crawford Long

In response to horror stories of bad medicine and botched medical treatment, trained doctors in the United States began to push for licensing laws. Such laws had existed in Europe since the 1200s. Medical practices in the United States gradually improved. Anesthetic made surgery less painful. In 1842, a young doctor named Crawford Long used ether—a clear liquid with a strong smell—as an anesthetic. By the 1880s, pain-free surgery was a standard for most operations.

The danger from infections during surgery had also been reduced. Joseph Lister, an English doctor and surgeon, found that keeping his hands, instruments, and operating room clean reduced the chance of infection in his patients. In 1867, he published his findings. American doctors who traveled to Europe for more training returned with information about Lister's discovery.

One of these American doctors was Charles H. Mayo, son of Dr. William Worrall Mayo. In 1889, Dr. Charles Mayo brought Lister's clean surgery methods from Europe to St. Mary's Hospital in Rochester, Minnesota. There, he and his brother, William James Mayo, operated and made many contributions to medical science.

Dr. Charles H. Mayo

Dr. William James Mayo

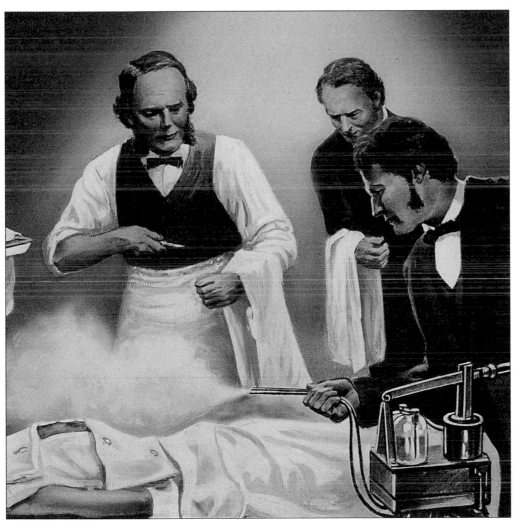

This painting shows Dr. Joseph Lister directing someone to clean a patient's wound during surgery.

Other doctors practicing in the American West discovered new methods of surgery. Dr. George Goodfellow of Tombstone, Arizona, took full advantage of Tombstone's reputation as a "town too tough to die." Living there gave Dr. Goodfellow a chance to operate on victims of gunfights, barroom brawls, and other accidents. The doctor shared his knowledge by publishing his surgical research.

By the time Dr. Goodfellow left Tombstone in 1891, the town's lawless days were almost over. Law, order, and boundaries were taking over the once wide open American West. Small settlements became towns with elected mayors. Towns became cities with elected councils and city services. Territories organized themselves into states, which then joined the United States. Open prairies became fenced farms and ranches where the laws of ownership applied.

Medicine also came under the rule of law. To help raise professional standards, the National Confederation of State Medical Examining and Licensing Boards was organized in 1891. The board worked to get medical licensing laws passed in each state. To practice medicine, a doctor had to meet certain standards of education and practical experience. To meet these new standards, doctors worked to open hospitals and medical schools in the American West.

By the 1890s, a number of hospitals and medical schools were in operation west of the Mississippi River. Some of these included St. Joseph's Hospital in Fort Worth, Texas, Toland Medical College in San Francisco, California, and the University of Oregon Medical School in Portland, Oregon.

Practicing medicine in the American West was difficult and dangerous. People who practiced medicine often could not make a living. But those who did accomplished two things that were very important to the future of the United States. They helped explore and develop the field of medicine as they explored and settled the American West.

This photograph of doctors and nurses at the Denver and Rio Grande Railroad Hospital was taken in the late 1800s.

GLOSSARY

amputate – to cut off a body part, such as an arm, leg, or finger, because it is damaged beyond repair

anesthetic – a gas or liquid drug given to someone before an operation to prevent pain

apprentice – a person who learns a trade or craft by working with a skilled person

bile – a thick, bitter fluid supplied by the liver to aid in digestion

contagious – spreading from one to another by direct or indirect contact

elixir – a liquid medicine with a sweet flavor

expedition – a journey made for a definite purpose or the group making such a journey

herb – a plant or plant part used in medicine or in seasoning foods

laboratory – a room or building in which experiments and tests are done

ointment – a thick, greasy medicine for use on the skin

patent – a document that gives the inventor of something the right to make, use, and sell the invention for a certain number of years

pharmacist – a trained person who prepares and sells drugs and medicines

prescribe – to order or direct the use of a medicine or treatment as a remedy

quack – a person who pretends to have medical knowledge or skill

symptom – evidence of an illness or bodily disorder

theory – a general rule offered to explain experiences or facts

tonic – a medicine that is supposed to make a person feel stronger or healthier

A young apprentice assists a doctor during surgery.

Patent medicine salespeople traveled in small wagons and sold medicines.

TIMELINE

1803 Louisiana Purchase

1804
⎱ Lewis and Clark Expedition
1806

1842 Dr. Crawford Long uses anesthetic on patient during surgery

California Gold Rush begins **1848**

American Civil War ⎰ **1861**
⎱ **1865**

1867 Dr. Joseph Lister publishes findings about cleanliness reducing infection

1889

Dr. Charles Mayo brings Lister's methods to St. Mary's Hospital

1891 Confederation of State Medical and Licensing Boards organized

INDEX (**Boldface** page numbers indicate illustrations.)

PHOTO CREDITS

Photographs ©: American Philosophical Society Library, Philadelphia: 6; Corbis-Bettmann: cover, 5, 9, 10, 11, 15, 16 top, 25, 27, 30, 31 center, 31 bottom; Denver Public Library, Western History Collection: 1, 8, 29; Liaison Agency, Inc./Hulton Getty: 20; Minnesota Historical Society: 12; Montana Historical Society, Helena/Don Beatty: 7; North Wind Picture Archives: 14, 19, 22, 23, 31 top; Stock Montage, Inc.: 2, 4, 26; Visuals Unlimited/Dick Keen: 16 bottom.

PHOTO IDENTIFICATIONS

Cover: This illustration shows a doctor giving medicine to a patient.
Page 1: Like most patent medicine salespeople, this man traveled in a small wagon and sold medicines from it.
Page 2: This illustration shows a medicine man selling his cures at a show in the 1800s.

ABOUT THE AUTHOR

Lucile Davis lives in Fort Worth, Texas. According to the city's newspaper, Fort Worth is "Where the West Begins." Ms. Davis is an author and teacher, and she serves on a number of boards, including The Friends of the Fort Worth Public Library and Tarrant County Historical Society. Ms. Davis is the author of several books for Children's Press: *The Mayo Brothers: Doctors to the World, R.J. Reynolds: He Saw the Future, Alabama,* and *Puerto Rico.*